Choosing a Mediterranean Lifestyle that will Improve Your Health

Follow the Mediterranean Diet

Sasha Merianelli

Table of Contents

Mushroom and Potato Oat Burgers

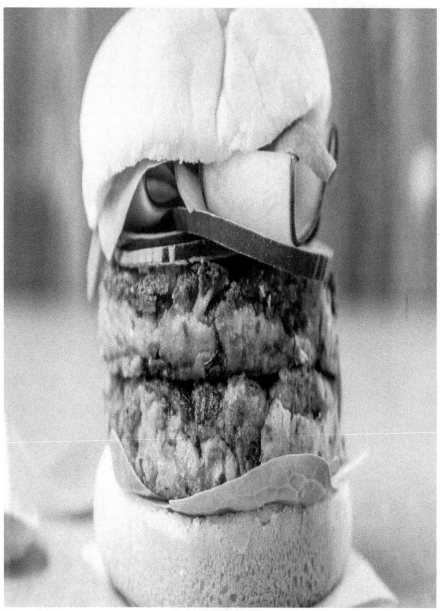

Prep time:

20 minutes | Cook time: 21 minutes | Serves 5

Ingredients

½ cup minced onion

1 teaspoon grated fresh ginger

½ cup minced mushrooms

½ cup red lentils, rinsed

¾ sweet potato, peeled and diced

1 cup vegetable stock

2 tablespoons hemp seeds

2 tablespoons chopped parsley

2 tablespoons chopped cilantro

1 tablespoon curry powder

1 cup quick oats

Brown rice flour, optional

5 tomato slices

Lettuce leaves

5 whole-wheat buns

Directions

1. Add the oil, ginger, mushrooms and onion into the instant pot and Sauté for 5 minutes.

2. Stir in the lentils, stock, and the sweet potatoes.

3. Secure the lid and cook on the Manual function for 6 minutes at High Pressure.

4. After the beep, natural release the pressure and remove the lid.

5. Meanwhile, heat the oven to 375°F (190°C) and line a baking tray with parchment paper.

6. Mash the prepared lentil mixture with a potato masher.

7. Add the oats and the remaining spices. Put in some brown rice flour if the mixture is not thick enough.

8. Wet your hands and prepare 5 patties, using the mixture, and place them on the baking tray.

9. Bake the patties for 10 minutes in the preheated oven.

10. Slice the buns in half and stack each with a tomato slice, a vegetable patty and lettuce leaves.

11. Serve and enjoy.

Per Serving

Calories: 266 | fat: 5.3g | protein: 14.5g | carbs: 48.7g | fiber: 9.6g | sodium: 276mg

Potato, Corn, and Spinach Medley

Prep time:

10 minutes | Cook time: 10 minutes | Serves 6

Ingredients

1 tablespoon olive oil

3 scallions, chopped

½ cup onion, chopped

2 large white potatoes, peeled and diced

1 tablespoon ginger, grated

3 cups frozen corn kernels

1 cup vegetable stock

1 tablespoon fish sauce

2 tablespoons light soy sauce

2 large cloves garlic, diced

⅓ teaspoon white pepper

1 teaspoon salt

3-4 handfuls baby spinach leaves

Juice of ½ lemon

Directions

1. Put the oil, ginger, garlic and onions in the instant pot and Sauté for 5 minutes.

2. Add all the remaining Ingredients except the spinach leaves and lime juice

3. Secure the lid and cook on the Manual setting for 5 minutes at High Pressure.

4. After the beep, Quick release the pressure and remove the lid.

5. Add the spinach and cook for 3 minutes on Sauté

6. Drizzle the lime juice over the dish and serve hot.

Per Serving

Calories: 217 | fat: 3.4g | protein: 6.5g | carbs: 44.5g | fiber: 6.3g | sodium: 892mg

Italian Zucchini Pomodoro

Prep time:

10 minutes | Cook time: 12 minutes | Serves 4

Ingredients

1 tablespoon avocado oil

1 large onion, peeled and diced

3 cloves garlic, minced

1 (28-ounce / 794-g) can diced tomatoes, including juice

½ cup water

1 tablespoon Italian seasoning

1 teaspoon sea salt

½ teaspoon ground black pepper

2 medium zucchini, spiraled

Directions

1. Press Sauté button on the Instant Pot. Heat avocado oil. Add onions and stir-fry for 3 to 5 minutes until translucent. Add garlic and cook for an additional minute. Add tomatoes, water, Italian seasoning, salt, and pepper. Add zucchini and toss to combine. Lock lid.

2. Press the Manual button and adjust time to 1 minute. When timer beeps, let pressure release naturally for 5 minutes. Quick release any additional pressure until float valve drops and then unlock lid.

3. Transfer zucchini to four bowls. Press Sauté button, press Adjust button to change the temperature to Less, and simmer sauce in the Instant Pot unlidded for 5 minutes. Ladle over zucchini and serve immediately.

Per Serving

Calories: 92 | fat: 4.1g | protein: 2.5g | carbs: 13.1g | fiber: 5.1g | sodium: 980mg

Mushroom Swoodles

Prep time:

5 minutes | Cook time: 3 minutes | Serves 4

Ingredients

2 tablespoons coconut aminos

1 tablespoon white vinegar

2 teaspoons olive oil

1 teaspoon sesame oil

1 tablespoon honey

¼ teaspoon red pepper flakes

3 cloves garlic, minced

1 large sweet potato, peeled and spiraled

1 pound (454 g) shiitake mushrooms, sliced

1 cup vegetable broth

¼ cup chopped fresh parsley

Directions

1. In a large bowl, whisk together coconut aminos, vinegar, olive oil, sesame oil, honey, red pepper flakes, and garlic.

2. Toss sweet potato and shiitake mushrooms in sauce. Refrigerate covered for 30 minutes.

3. Pour vegetable broth into Instant Pot. Add trivet. Lower steamer basket onto trivet and add the sweet potato mixture to the basket. Lock lid.

4. Press the Manual button and adjust time to 3 minutes. When timer beeps, let pressure release naturally for 5 minutes. Quick release any additional pressure until float valve drops and then unlock lid.

5. Remove basket from the Instant Pot and distribute sweet potatoes and mushrooms evenly among four bowls; pour liquid from the Instant Pot over bowls and garnish with chopped parsley.

Per Serving

Calories: 127 | fat: 4.0g | protein: 4.2g | carbs: 20.9g | fiber: 4.1g | sodium: 671mg

Rice, Corn, and Bean Stuffed Peppers

Prep time:

15 minutes | Cook time: 15 minutes | Serves 4

Ingredients

4 large bell peppers

2 cups cooked white rice

1 medium onion, peeled and diced

3 small Roma tomatoes, diced

¼ cup marinara sauce

1 cup corn kernels (cut from the cob is preferred)

¼ cup sliced black olives

¼ cup canned cannellini beans, rinsed and drained

¼ cup canned black beans, rinsed and drained

1 teaspoon sea salt

1 teaspoon garlic powder

½ cup vegetable broth

2 tablespoons grated Parmesan cheese

Directions

1. Cut off the bell pepper tops as close to the tops as possible. Hollow out and discard seeds. Poke a few small holes in the bottom of the peppers to allow drippings to drain.

2. In a medium bowl, combine remaining Ingredients except for broth and Parmesan cheese. Stuff equal amounts of mixture into each of the bell peppers.

3. Place trivet into the Instant Pot and pour in the broth. Set the peppers upright on the trivet. Lock lid.

4. Press the Manual button and adjust time to 15 minutes. When timer beeps, let pressure release naturally until float valve drops and then unlock lid.

5. Serve immediately and garnish with Parmesan cheese.

Per Serving

Calories: 265 | fat: 3.0g | protein: 8.1g | carbs: 53.1g | fiber: 8.0g | sodium: 834mg

Carrot and Turnip Purée

Prep time:

10 minutes | Cook time: 10 minutes | Serves 6

Ingredients

2 tablespoons olive oil, divided

3 large turnips, peeled and quartered

4 large carrots, peeled and cut into 2-inch pieces

2 cups vegetable broth

1 teaspoon salt

½ teaspoon ground nutmeg

2 tablespoons sour cream

Directions

1. Press the Sauté button on Instant Pot. Heat 1 tablespoon olive oil. Toss turnips and carrots in oil for 1 minute. Add broth. Lock lid.

2. Press the Manual button and adjust time to 8 minutes. When timer beeps, quick release pressure until float valve drops and then unlock lid.

3. Drain vegetables and reserve liquid; set liquid aside. Add 2 tablespoons of reserved liquid plus remaining Ingredients to vegetables in the Instant Pot. Use an immersion blender to blend until desired smoothness. If too thick, add more liquid 1 tablespoon at a time. Serve warm.

Per Serving

Calories: 95 | fat: 5.2g | protein: 1.4g | carbs: 11.8g | fiber: 3.0g | sodium: 669mg

Brussels Sprouts Linguine

Prep time:

5 minutes | Cook time: 25 minutes | Serves 4

Ingredients

8 ounces (227 g) whole-wheat linguine

⅓ cup plus 2 tablespoons extra-virgin olive oil, divided

1 medium sweet onion, diced

2 to 3 garlic cloves, smashed

8 ounces (227 g) Brussels sprouts, chopped

½ cup chicken stock

⅓ cup dry white wine

½ cup shredded Parmesan cheese

1 lemon, quartered

Directions

1. Bring a large pot of water to a boil and cook the pasta for about 5 minutes, or until al dente. Drain the pasta and reserve 1 cup of the pasta water. Mix the cooked pasta with 2 tablespoons of the olive oil. Set aside.

2. In a large skillet, heat the remaining ⅓ cup of the olive oil over medium heat. Add the onion to the skillet and sauté for about 4 minutes, or until tender. Add the smashed garlic cloves and sauté for 1 minute, or until fragrant.

3. Stir in the Brussels sprouts and cook covered for 10 minutes. Pour in the chicken stock to prevent burning. Once the Brussels sprouts have wilted and are fork-tender, add white wine and cook for about 5 minutes, or until reduced.

4. Add the pasta to the skillet and add the pasta water as needed.

5. Top with the Parmesan cheese and squeeze the lemon over the dish right before eating.

Per Serving

Calories: 502 | fat: 31.0g | protein: 15.0g | carbs: 50.0g | fiber: 9.0g | sodium: 246mg

Beet and Watercress Salad

Prep time:

15 minutes | Cook time: 8 minutes | Serves 4

Ingredients

2 pounds (907 g) beets, scrubbed, trimmed and cut into ¾-inch pieces

½ cup water

1 teaspoon caraway seeds

½ teaspoon table salt, plus more for seasoning

1 cup plain Greek yogurt

1 small garlic clove, minced

5 ounces (142 g) watercress, torn into bite-size pieces

1 tablespoon extra-virgin olive oil, divided, plus more for drizzling

1 tablespoon white wine vinegar, divided

Black pepper, to taste

1 teaspoon grated orange zest

2 tablespoons orange juice

¼ cup coarsely chopped fresh dill

¼ cup hazelnuts, toasted, skinned and chopped

Coarse sea salt, to taste

Directions

1. Combine the beets, water, caraway seeds and table salt in the Instant Pot. Set the lid in place. Select the Manual mode and set the cooking time for 8 minutes on High Pressure. When the timer goes off, do a quick pressure release.

2. Carefully open the lid. Using a slotted spoon, transfer the beets to a plate. Set aside to cool slightly.

3. In a small bowl, combine the yogurt, garlic and 3 tablespoons of the beet cooking liquid. In a large bowl, toss the watercress with 2 teaspoons of the oil and 1 teaspoon of the vinegar. Season with table salt and pepper.

4. Spread the yogurt mixture over a serving dish. Arrange the watercress on top of the yogurt mixture, leaving 1-inch border of the yogurt mixture.

5. Add the beets to now-empty large bowl and toss with the orange zest and juice, the remaining 2 teaspoons of the vinegar and the remaining 1 teaspoon of the oil. Season with table salt and pepper.

6. Arrange the beets on top of the watercress mixture. Drizzle with the olive oil and sprinkle with the dill, hazelnuts and sea salt.

7. Serve immediately.

Per Serving

Calories: 240 | fat: 15.0g | protein: 9.0g | carbs: 19.0g | fiber: 5.0g | sodium: 440mg

Garlicky Broccoli Rabe

Prep time:

10 minutes | Cook time: 5 to 6 minutes | Serves 4

25

Ingredients

14 ounces (397 g) broccoli rabe, trimmed and cut into 1-inch pieces

2 teaspoons salt, plus more for seasoning

Black pepper, to taste

2 tablespoons extra-virgin olive oil

3 garlic cloves, minced

¼ teaspoon red pepper flakes

Directions

1. Bring 3 quarts water to a boil in a large saucepan. Add the broccoli rabe and 2 teaspoons of the salt to the boiling water and cook for 2 to 3 minutes, or until wilted and tender.

2. Drain the broccoli rabe. Transfer to ice water and let sit until chilled. Drain again and pat dry.

3. In a skillet over medium heat, heat the oil and add the garlic and red pepper flakes. Sauté for about 2 minutes, or until the garlic begins to sizzle.

4. Increase the heat to medium-high. Stir in the broccoli rabe and cook for about 1 minute, or until heated through, stirring constantly. Season with salt and pepper.

5. Serve immediately.

Per Serving

Calories: 87 | fat: 7.3g | protein: 3.4g | carbs: 4.0g | fiber: 2.9g | sodium: 1196mg

Sautéed Cabbage with Parsley

Prep time:

10 minutes | Cook time: 12 to 14 minutes | Serves 4 to 6

Ingredients

1 small head green cabbage (about 1¼ pounds / 567 g), cored and sliced thin

2 tablespoons extra-virgin olive oil, divided

1 onion, halved and sliced thin

¾ teaspoon salt, divided

¼ teaspoon black pepper

¼ cup chopped fresh parsley

1½ teaspoons lemon juice

Directions

1. Place the cabbage in a large bowl with cold water. Let sit for 3 minutes. Drain well.

2. Heat 1 tablespoon of the oil in a skillet over medium-high heat until shimmering. Add the onion and ¼ teaspoon of the salt and cook for 5 to 7 minutes, or until softened and lightly browned. Transfer to a bowl.

3. Heat the remaining 1 tablespoon of the oil in now-empty skillet over medium-high heat until shimmering. Add the cabbage and sprinkle with the remaining ½ teaspoon of the salt and black pepper. Cover and cook for about 3 minutes, without stirring, or until cabbage is wilted and lightly browned on bottom.

4. Stir and continue to cook for about 4 minutes, uncovered, or until the cabbage is crisp-tender and lightly browned in places, stirring once halfway through cooking. Off heat, stir in the cooked onion, parsley and lemon juice.

5. Transfer to a plate and serve.

Per Serving

Calories: 117 | fat: 7.0g | protein: 2.7g | carbs: 13.4g | fiber: 5.1g | sodium: 472mg

Braised Cauliflower with White Wine

Prep time:

10 minutes | Cook time: 12 to 16 minutes | Serves 4 to 6

Ingredients

3 tablespoons plus 1 teaspoon extra-virgin olive oil, divided

3 garlic cloves, minced

⅛ teaspoon red pepper flakes

1 head cauliflower (2 pounds / 907 g), cored and cut into 1½-inch florets

¼ teaspoon salt, plus more for seasoning

Black pepper, to taste

⅓ cup vegetable broth

⅓ cup dry white wine

2 tablespoons minced fresh parsley

Directions

1. Combine 1 teaspoon of the oil, garlic and pepper flakes in small bowl.

2. Heat the remaining 3 tablespoons of the oil in a skillet over medium-high heat until shimmering. Add the cauliflower and ¼ teaspoon of the salt and cook for 7 to 9 minutes, stirring occasionally, or until florets are golden brown.

3. Push the cauliflower to sides of the skillet. Add the garlic mixture to the center of the skillet. Cook for about 30 seconds, or until fragrant. Stir the garlic mixture into the cauliflower.

4. Pour in the broth and wine and bring to simmer. Reduce the heat to medium-low. Cover and cook for 4 to 6 minutes, or until the cauliflower is crisp-tender. Off heat, stir in the parsley and season with salt and pepper.

5. Serve immediately.

Per Serving

Calories: 143 | fat: 11.7g | protein: 3.1g | carbs: 8.7g | fiber: 3.1g | sodium: 263mg

Cauliflower Steaks with Arugula

Prep time:

5 minutes | Cook time: 20 minutes | Serves 4

Ingredients

Cauliflower:

1 head cauliflower

Cooking spray

½ teaspoon garlic powder

4 cups arugula

Dressing:

1½ tablespoons extra-virgin olive oil

1½ tablespoons honey mustard

1 teaspoon freshly squeezed lemon juice

Directions

1. Preheat the oven to 425°F (220°C).

2. Remove the leaves from the cauliflower head, and cut it in half lengthwise. Cut 1½-inch-thick steaks from each half.

3. Spritz both sides of each steak with cooking spray and season both sides with the garlic powder.

4. Place the cauliflower steaks on a baking sheet, cover with foil, and roast in the oven for 10 minutes.

5. Remove the baking sheet from the oven and gently pull back the foil to avoid the steam. Flip the steaks, then roast uncovered for 10 minutes more.

6. Meanwhile, make the dressing: Whisk together the olive oil, honey mustard and lemon juice in a small bowl.

7. When the cauliflower steaks are done, divide into four equal portions. Top each portion with one-quarter of the arugula and dressing.

8. Serve immediately.

Per Serving

Calories: 115 | fat: 6.0g | protein: 5.0g | carbs: 14.0g | fiber: 4.0g | sodium: 97mg

Parmesan Stuffed Zucchini Boats

Prep time:

5 minutes | Cook time: 15 minutes | Serves 4

Ingredients

1 cup canned low-sodium chickpeas, drained and rinsed

1 cup no-sugar-added spaghetti sauce

2 zucchinis

¼ cup shredded Parmesan cheese

Directions

1. Preheat the oven to 425°F (220°C).

2. In a medium bowl, stir together the chickpeas and spaghetti sauce.

3. Cut the zucchini in half lengthwise and scrape a spoon gently down the length of each half to remove the seeds.

4. Fill each zucchini half with the chickpea sauce and top with one-quarter of the Parmesan cheese.

5. Place the zucchini halves on a baking sheet and roast in the oven for 15 minutes.

6. Transfer to a plate. Let rest for 5 minutes before serving.

Per Serving

Calories: 139 | fat: 4.0g | protein: 8.0g | carbs: 20.0g | fiber: 5.0g | sodium: 344mg

Baby Kale and Cabbage Salad

Prep time:

10 minutes | Cook time: 0 minutes | Serves 6

Ingredients

2 bunches baby kale, thinly sliced

½ head green savoy cabbage, cored and thinly sliced

1 medium red bell pepper, thinly sliced

1 garlic clove, thinly sliced

1 cup toasted peanuts

Dressing:

Juice of 1 lemon

¼ cup apple cider vinegar

1 teaspoon ground cumin

¼ teaspoon smoked paprika

Directions

1. In a large mixing bowl, toss together the kale and cabbage.

2. Make the dressing: Whisk together the lemon juice, vinegar, cumin and paprika in a small bowl.

3. Pour the dressing over the greens and gently massage with your hands.

4. Add the pepper, garlic and peanuts to the mixing bowl. Toss to combine.

5. Serve immediately.

Per Serving

Calories: 199 | fat: 12.0g | protein: 10.0g | carbs: 17.0g | fiber: 5.0g | sodium: 46mg

Grilled Romaine Lettuce

Prep time:

5 minutes | Cook time: 3 to 5 minutes | Serves 4

Ingredients

Romaine:

2 heads romaine lettuce, halved lengthwise

2 tablespoons extra-virgin olive oil

Dressing:

½ cup unsweetened almond milk

1 tablespoon extra-virgin olive oil

¼ bunch fresh chives, thinly chopped

1 garlic clove, pressed

1 pinch red pepper flakes

Directions

1. Heat a grill pan over medium heat.

2. Brush each lettuce half with the olive oil. Place the lettuce halves, flat-side down, on the grill. Grill for 3 to 5 minutes, or until the lettuce slightly wilts and develops light grill marks.

3. Meanwhile, whisk together all the Ingredients for the dressing in a small bowl.

4. Drizzle 2 tablespoons of the dressing over each romaine half and serve.

Per Serving

Calories: 126 | fat: 11.0g | protein: 2.0g | carbs: 7.0g | fiber: 1.0g | sodium: 41mg

Mini Crustless Spinach Quiches

Prep time:

10 minutes | Cook time: 20 minutes | Serves 6

Ingredients

2 tablespoons extra-virgin olive oil

1 onion, finely chopped

2 cups baby spinach

2 garlic cloves, minced

8 large eggs, beaten

¼ cup unsweetened almond milk

½ teaspoon sea salt

¼ teaspoon freshly ground black pepper

1 cup shredded Swiss cheese

Cooking spray

Directions

1. Preheat the oven to 375°F (190°C). Spritz a 6-cup muffin tin with cooking spray. Set aside.

2. In a large skillet over medium-high heat, heat the olive oil until shimmering. Add the onion and cook for about 4 minutes, or until soft. Add the spinach and cook for about 1 minute, stirring constantly, or until the spinach softens. Add the garlic and sauté for 30 seconds. Remove from the heat and let cool.

3. In a medium bowl, whisk together the eggs, milk, salt and pepper.

4. Stir the cooled vegetables and the cheese into the egg mixture. Spoon the mixture into the prepared muffin tins. Bake for about 15 minutes, or until the eggs are set.

5. Let rest for 5 minutes before serving.

Per Serving

Calories: 218 | fat: 17.0g | protein: 14.0g | carbs: 4.0g | fiber: 1.0g | sodium: 237mg

Butternut Noodles with Mushrooms

Prep time:

10 minutes | Cook time: 12 minutes | Serves 4

Ingredients

¼ cup extra-virgin olive oil

1 pound (454 g) cremini mushrooms, sliced

½ red onion, finely chopped

1 teaspoon dried thyme

½ teaspoon sea salt

3 garlic cloves, minced

½ cup dry white wine

Pinch of red pepper flakes

4 cups butternut noodles

4 ounces (113 g) grated Parmesan cheese

Directions

1. In a large skillet over medium-high heat, heat the olive oil until shimmering. Add the mushrooms, onion, thyme, and salt to the skillet. Cook for about 6 minutes, stirring occasionally, or until the mushrooms start to brown. Add the garlic and sauté for 30 seconds. Stir in the white wine and red pepper flakes.

2. Fold in the noodles. Cook for about 5 minutes, stirring occasionally, or until the noodles are tender.

3. Serve topped with the grated Parmesan.

Per Serving

Calories: 244 | fat: 14.0g | protein: 4.0g | carbs: 22.0g | fiber: 4.0g | sodium: 159mg

Potato Tortilla with Leeks and Mushrooms

Prep time:

30 minutes | Cook time: 50 minutes | Serves 2

Ingredients

1 tablespoon olive oil

1 cup thinly sliced leeks

4 ounces (113 g) baby bella (cremini) mushrooms, stemmed and sliced

1 small potato, peeled and sliced ¼-inch thick

½ cup unsweetened almond milk

5 large eggs, beaten

1 teaspoon Dijon mustard

½ teaspoon salt

½ teaspoon dried thyme

Pinch freshly ground black pepper

3 ounces (85 g) Gruyère cheese, shredded

Directions

1. Preheat the oven to 350°F (180°C).

2. In a large sauté pan over medium-high heat, heat the olive oil. Add the leeks, mushrooms, and potato and sauté for about 10 minutes, or until the potato starts to brown.

3. Reduce the heat to medium-low, cover, and cook for an additional 10 minutes, or until the potato begins to soften. Add 1 to 2 tablespoons of water to prevent sticking to the bottom of the pan, if needed.

4. Meanwhile, whisk together the milk, beaten eggs, mustard, salt, thyme, black pepper, and cheese in a medium bowl until combined.

5. When the potatoes are fork-tender, turn off the heat.

6. Transfer the cooked vegetables to an oiled nonstick ovenproof pan and arrange them in a nice layer along the bottom and slightly up the sides of the pan. Pour the milk mixture evenly over the vegetables.

7. Bake in the preheated oven for 25 to 30 minutes, or until the eggs are completely set and the top is golden and puffed.

8. Remove from the oven and cool for 5 minutes before cutting and serving.

Per Serving

Calories: 541 | fat: 33.1g | protein: 32.8g | carbs: 31.0g | fiber: 4.0g | sodium: 912mg

Mushrooms Ragu with Cheesy Polenta

Prep time:

20 minutes | Cook time: 30 minutes | Serves 2

Ingredients

½ ounce (14 g) dried porcini mushrooms

1 pound (454 g) baby bella (cremini) mushrooms, quartered

2 tablespoons olive oil

1 garlic clove, minced

1 large shallot, minced

1 tablespoon flour

2 teaspoons tomato paste

½ cup red wine

1 cup mushroom stock (or reserved liquid from soaking the porcini mushrooms, if using)

1 fresh rosemary sprig

½ teaspoon dried thyme

1½ cups water

½ teaspoon salt, plus more as needed

⅓ cup instant polenta

2 tablespoons grated Parmesan cheese

Directions

1. Soak the dried porcini mushrooms in 1 cup of hot water for about 15 minutes to soften them. When ready, scoop them out of the water, reserving the soaking liquid. Mince the porcini mushrooms.

2. Heat the olive oil in a large sauté pan over medium-high heat. Add the mushrooms, garlic, and shallot and sauté for 10 minutes, or until the vegetables are beginning to caramelize.

3. Stir in the flour and tomato paste and cook for an additional 30 seconds. Add the red wine, mushroom stock, rosemary, and thyme. Bring the mixture to a boil, stirring constantly, or until it has thickened.

4. Reduce the heat and allow to simmer for 10 minutes.

5. Meanwhile, bring the water to a boil in a saucepan and sprinkle with the salt.

6. Add the instant polenta and stir quickly while it thickens. Scatter with the grated Parmesan cheese. Taste and season with more salt as needed. Serve warm.

Per Serving

Calories: 450 | fat: 16.0g | protein: 14.1g | carbs: 57.8g | fiber: 5.0g | sodium: 165mg

Veggie Rice Bowls with Pesto Sauce

Prep time:

15 minutes | Cook time: 1 minute | Serves 2

Ingredients

2 cups water

1 cup arborio rice, rinsed

Salt and ground black pepper, to taste

2 eggs

1 cup broccoli florets

½ pound (227 g) Brussels sprouts

1 carrot, peeled and chopped

1 small beet, peeled and cubed

¼ cup pesto sauce

Lemon wedges, for serving

Directions

1. Combine the water, rice, salt, and pepper in the Instant Pot. Insert a trivet over rice and place a steamer basket on top. Add the eggs, broccoli, Brussels sprouts, carrots, beet cubes, salt, and pepper to the steamer basket.

2. Lock the lid. Select the Manual mode and set the cooking time for 1 minute at High Pressure.

3. When the timer beeps, perform a natural pressure release for 10 minutes, then release any remaining pressure. Carefully open the lid.

4. Remove the steamer basket and trivet from the pot and transfer the eggs to a bowl of ice water. Peel and halve the eggs. Use a fork to fluff the rice.

5. Divide the rice, broccoli, Brussels sprouts, carrot, beet cubes, and eggs into two bowls. Top with a dollop of pesto sauce and serve with the lemon wedges.

Per Serving

Calories: 590 | fat: 34.1g | protein: 21.9g | carbs: 50.0g | fiber: 19.6g | sodium: 670mg

Roasted Cauliflower and Carrots

Prep time:

10 minutes | Cook time: 30 minutes | Serves 2

Ingredients

4 cups cauliflower florets (about ½ small head)

2 medium carrots, peeled, halved, and then sliced into quarters lengthwise

2 tablespoons olive oil, divided

½ teaspoon salt, divided

½ teaspoon garlic powder, divided

2 teaspoons za'atar spice mix, divided

1 (15-ounce / 425-g) can chickpeas, drained, rinsed, and patted dry

¾ cup plain Greek yogurt

1 teaspoon harissa spice paste, plus additional as needed

Directions

1. Preheat the oven to 400°F (205°C). Line a sheet pan with foil or parchment paper.

2. Put the cauliflower and carrots in a large bowl. Drizzle with 1 tablespoon of olive oil and sprinkle with ¼ teaspoon of salt, ¼ teaspoon of garlic powder, and 1 teaspoon of za'atar. Toss to combine well.

3. Spread the vegetables onto one half of the prepared sheet pan in a single layer.

4. Put the chickpeas in the same bowl and season with the remaining 1 tablespoon of olive oil, ¼ teaspoon of salt, ¼ teaspoon of garlic powder, and the remaining 1 teaspoon of za'atar. Toss to combine well.

5. Spread the chickpeas onto the other half of the sheet pan.

6. Roast in the preheated oven for 30 minutes, or until the vegetables are crisp-tender. Flip the vegetables halfway through and give the chickpeas a stir so they cook evenly.

7. Meanwhile, whisk the yogurt and harissa together in a small bowl. Taste and add additional harissa as needed.

8. Serve the vegetables and chickpeas with the yogurt mixture on the side.

Per Serving

Calories: 468 | fat: 23.0g | protein: 18.1g | carbs: 54.1g | fiber: 13.8g | sodium: 631mg

Sautéed Spinach and Leeks

Prep time:

5 minutes | Cook time: 8 minutes | Serves 2

Ingredients

3 tablespoons olive oil

2 garlic cloves, crushed

2 leeks, chopped

2 red onions, chopped

9 ounces (255 g) fresh spinach

1 teaspoon kosher salt

½ cup crumbled goat cheese

Directions

1. Coat the bottom of the Instant Pot with the olive oil.

2. Add the garlic, leek, and onions and stir-fry for about 5 minutes, on Sauté mode.

3. Stir in the spinach. Sprinkle with the salt and sauté for an additional 3 minutes, stirring constantly.

4. Transfer to a plate and scatter with the goat cheese before serving.

Per Serving

Calories: 447 | fat: 31.2g | protein: 14.6g | carbs: 28.7g | fiber: 6.3g | sodium: 937mg

Zoodles with Beet Pesto

Prep time:

10 minutes | Cook time: 50 minutes | Serves 2

Ingredients

1 medium red beet, peeled, chopped

½ cup walnut pieces

½ cup crumbled goat cheese

3 garlic cloves

2 tablespoons freshly squeezed lemon juice

2 tablespoons plus 2 teaspoons extra-virgin olive oil, divided

¼ teaspoon salt

4 small zucchinis, spiralized

Directions

1. Preheat the oven to 375°F (190°C).

2. Wrap the chopped beet in a piece of aluminum foil and seal well.

3. Roast in the preheated oven for 30 to 40 minutes until tender.

4. Meanwhile, heat a skillet over medium-high heat until hot. Add the walnuts and toast for 5 to 7 minutes, or until fragrant and lightly browned.

5. Remove the cooked beets from the oven and place in a food processor. Add the toasted walnuts, goat cheese, garlic, lemon juice, 2 tablespoons of olive oil, and salt. Pulse until smoothly blended. Set aside.

6. Heat the remaining 2 teaspoons of olive oil in a large skillet over medium heat. Add the zucchini and toss to coat in the oil. Cook for 2 to 3 minutes, stirring gently, or until the zucchini is softened.

7. Transfer the zucchini to a serving plate and toss with the beet pesto, then serve.

Per Serving

Calories: 423 | fat: 38.8g | protein: 8.0g | carbs: 17.1g | fiber: 6.0g | sodium: 338mg

Fried Eggplant Rolls

Prep time:

20 minutes | Cook time: 10 minutes | Serves 4 to 6

Ingredients

1 large eggplants, trimmed and cut lengthwise into ¼-inch-thick slices

1 teaspoon salt

1 cup ricotta cheese

4 ounces (113 g) goat cheese, shredded

¼ cup finely chopped fresh basil

½ teaspoon freshly ground black pepper

Olive oil spray

Directions

1. Add the eggplant slices to a colander and season with salt. Set aside for 15 to 20 minutes.

2. Mix together the ricotta and goat cheese, basil, and black pepper in a large bowl and stir to combine. Set aside.

3. Dry the eggplant slices with paper towels and lightly mist them with olive oil spray.

4. Heat a large skillet over medium heat and lightly spray it with olive oil spray.

5. Arrange the eggplant slices in the skillet and fry each side for 3 minutes until golden brown.

6. Remove from the heat to a paper towel-lined plate and rest for 5 minutes.

7. Make the eggplant rolls: Lay the eggplant slices on a flat work surface and top each slice with a tablespoon of the prepared cheese mixture. Roll them up and serve immediately.

Per Serving

Calories: 254 | fat: 14.9g | protein: 15.3g | carbs: 18.6g | fiber: 7.1g | sodium: 745mg

Roasted Veggies and Brown Rice Bowl

Prep time:

15 minutes | Cook time: 20 minutes | Serves 4

Ingredients

2 cups cauliflower florets

2 cups broccoli florets

1 (15-ounce / 425-g) can chickpeas, drained and rinsed

1 cup carrot slices (about 1 inch thick)

2 to 3 tablespoons extra-virgin olive oil, divided

Salt and freshly ground black pepper, to taste

Nonstick cooking spray

2 cups cooked brown rice

2 to 3 tablespoons sesame seeds, for garnish

Dressing:

3 to 4 tablespoons tahini

2 tablespoons honey

1 lemon, juiced

1 garlic clove, minced

Salt and freshly ground black pepper, to taste

Directions

1. Preheat the oven to 400°F (205°C). Spritz two baking sheets with nonstick cooking spray.

2. Spread the cauliflower and broccoli on the first baking sheet and the second with the chickpeas and carrot slices.

3. Drizzle each sheet with half of the olive oil and sprinkle with salt and pepper. Toss to coat well.

4. Roast the chickpeas and carrot slices in the preheated oven for 10 minutes, leaving the carrots tender but crisp, and the cauliflower and broccoli for 20 minutes until fork-tender. Stir them once halfway through the cooking time.

5. Meanwhile, make the dressing: Whisk together the tahini, honey, lemon juice, garlic, salt, and pepper in a small bowl.

6. Divide the cooked brown rice among four bowls. Top each bowl evenly with roasted vegetables and dressing. Sprinkle the sesame seeds on top for garnish before serving.

Per Serving

Calories: 453 | fat: 17.8g | protein: 12.1g | carbs: 61.8g | fiber: 11.2g | sodium: 60mg

Cauliflower Hash with Carrots

Prep time:

10 minutes | Cook time: 10 minutes | Serves 4

Ingredients

3 tablespoons extra-virgin olive oil

1 large onion, chopped

1 tablespoon minced garlic

2 cups diced carrots

4 cups cauliflower florets

½ teaspoon ground cumin

1 teaspoon salt

Directions

1. In a large skillet, heat the olive oil over medium heat.

2. Add the onion and garlic and sauté for 1 minute. Stir in the carrots and stir-fry for 3 minutes.

3. Add the cauliflower florets, cumin, and salt and toss to combine.

4. Cover and cook for 3 minutes until lightly browned. Stir well and cook, uncovered, for 3 to 4 minutes, until softened.

5. Remove from the heat and serve warm.

Per Serving

Calories: 158 | fat: 10.8g | protein: 3.1g | carbs: 14.9g | fiber: 5.1g | sodium: 656mg

Garlicky Zucchini Cubes with Mint

Prep time:

5 minutes | Cook time: 10 minutes | Serves 4

Ingredients

3 large green zucchini, cut into ½-inch cubes

3 tablespoons extra-virgin olive oil

1 large onion, chopped

3 cloves garlic, minced

1 teaspoon salt

1 teaspoon dried mint

Directions

1. Heat the olive oil in a large skillet over medium heat.

2. Add the onion and garlic and sauté for 3 minutes, stirring constantly, or until softened.

3. Stir in the zucchini cubes and salt and cook for 5 minutes, or until the zucchini is browned and tender.

4. Add the mint to the skillet and toss to combine, then continue cooking for 2 minutes.

5. Serve warm.

Per Serving

Calories: 146 | fat: 10.6g | protein: 4.2g | carbs: 11.8g | fiber: 3.0g | sodium: 606mg

Zucchini and Artichokes Bowl with Farro

Prep time:

15 minutes | Cook time: 10 minutes | Serves 4 to 6

Ingredients

⅓ cup extra-virgin olive oil

⅓ cup chopped red onions

½ cup chopped red bell pepper

2 garlic cloves, minced

1 cup zucchini, cut into ½-inch-thick slices

½ cup coarsely chopped artichokes

½ cup canned chickpeas, drained and rinsed

3 cups cooked farro

Salt and freshly ground black pepper, to taste

½ cup crumbled feta cheese, for serving (optional)

¼ cup sliced olives, for serving (optional)

2 tablespoons fresh basil, chiffonade, for serving (optional)

3 tablespoons balsamic vinegar, for serving (optional)

Directions

1. Heat the olive oil in a large skillet over medium heat until it shimmers.

2. Add the onions, bell pepper, and garlic and sauté for 5 minutes, stirring occasionally, until softened.

3. Stir in the zucchini slices, artichokes, and chickpeas and sauté for about 5 minutes until slightly tender.

4. Add the cooked farro and toss to combine until heated through. Sprinkle the salt and pepper to season.

5. Divide the mixture into bowls. Top each bowl evenly with feta cheese, olive slices, and basil and sprinkle with the balsamic vinegar, if desired.

Per Serving

Calories: 366 | fat: 19.9g | protein: 9.3g | carbs: 50.7g | fiber: 9.0g | sodium: 86mg

Zucchini Fritters

Prep time:

15 minutes | Cook time: 5 minutes | Makes 14 fritters

Ingredients

4 cups grated zucchini

Salt, to taste

2 large eggs, lightly beaten

⅓ cup sliced scallions (green and white parts)

⅔ all-purpose flour

⅛ teaspoon black pepper

2 tablespoons olive oil

Directions

1. Put the grated zucchini in a colander and lightly season with salt. Set aside to rest for 10 minutes. Squeeze out as much liquid from the grated zucchini as possible.

2. Pour the grated zucchini into a bowl. Fold in the beaten eggs, scallions, flour, salt, and pepper and stir until everything is well combined.

3. Heat the olive oil in a large skillet over medium heat until hot.

4. Drop 3 tablespoons mounds of the zucchini mixture onto the hot skillet to make each fritter, pressing them lightly into rounds and spacing them about 2 inches apart.

5. Cook for 2 to 3 minutes. Flip the zucchini fritters and cook for 2 minutes more, or until they are golden brown and cooked through.

6. Remove from the heat to a plate lined with paper towels. Repeat with the remaining zucchini mixture.

7. Serve hot.

Per Serving (2 fritters)

Calories: 113 | fat: 6.1g | protein: 4.0g | carbs: 12.2g | fiber: 1.0g | sodium: 25mg

Moroccan Tagine with Vegetables

Prep time:

20 minutes | Cook time: 40 minutes | Serves 2

Ingredients

2 tablespoons olive oil

½ onion, diced

1 garlic clove, minced

2 cups cauliflower florets

1 medium carrot, cut into 1-inch pieces

1 cup diced eggplant

1 (28-ounce / 794-g) can whole tomatoes with their juices

1 (15-ounce / 425-g) can chickpeas, drained and rinsed

2 small red potatoes, cut into 1-inch pieces

1 cup water

1 teaspoon pure maple syrup

½ teaspoon cinnamon

½ teaspoon turmeric

1 teaspoon cumin

½ teaspoon salt

1 to 2 teaspoons harissa paste

Directions

1. In a Dutch oven, heat the olive oil over medium-high heat. Saut é the onion for 5 minutes, stirring occasionally, or until the onion is translucent.

2. Stir in the garlic, cauliflower florets, carrot, eggplant, tomatoes, and potatoes. Using a wooden spoon or spatula to break up the tomatoes into smaller pieces.

3. Add the chickpeas, water, maple syrup, cinnamon, turmeric, cumin, and salt and stir to incorporate. Bring the mixture to a boil.

4. Once it starts to boil, reduce the heat to medium-low. Stir in the harissa paste, cover, allow to simmer for about 40 minutes, or until the vegetables are softened. Taste and adjust seasoning as needed.

5. Let the mixture cool for 5 minutes before serving.

Per Serving

Calories: 293 | fat: 9.9g | protein: 11.2g | carbs: 45.5g | fiber: 12.1g | sodium: 337mg

Vegan Lentil Bolognese

Prep time:

15 minutes | Cook time: 50 minutes | Serves 2

Ingredients

1 medium celery stalk

1 large carrot

½ large onion

1 garlic clove

2 tablespoons olive oil

1 (28-ounce / 794-g) can crushed tomatoes

1 cup red wine

½ teaspoon salt, plus more as needed

½ teaspoon pure maple syrup

1 cup cooked lentils (prepared from ½ cup dry)

Directions

1. Add the celery, carrot, onion, and garlic to a food processor and process until everything is finely chopped.

2. In a Dutch oven, heat the olive oil over medium-high heat. Add the chopped mixture and saut é for about 10 minutes, stirring occasionally, or until the vegetables are lightly browned.

3. Stir in the tomatoes, wine, salt, and maple syrup and bring to a boil.

4. Once the sauce starts to boil, cover, and reduce the heat to medium-low. Simmer for 30 minutes, stirring occasionally, or until the vegetables are softened.

5. Stir in the cooked lentils and cook for an additional 5 minutes until warmed through.

6. Taste and add additional salt, if needed. Serve warm.

Per Serving

Calories: 367 | fat: 15.0g | protein: 13.7g | carbs: 44.5g | fiber: 17.6g | sodium: 1108mg

Grilled Vegetable Skewers

Prep time:

15 minutes | Cook time: 10 minutes | Serves 4

Ingredients

4 medium red onions, peeled and sliced into 6 wedges

4 medium zucchinis, cut into 1-inch-thick slices

2 beefsteak tomatoes, cut into quarters

4 red bell peppers, cut into 2-inch squares

2 orange bell peppers, cut into 2-inch squares

2 yellow bell peppers, cut into 2-inch squares

2 tablespoons plus

1 teaspoon olive oil, divided

Special Equipment:

4 wooden skewers, soaked in water for at least 30 minutes

Directions

1. Preheat the grill to medium-high heat.

2. Skewer the vegetables by alternating between red onion, zucchini, tomatoes, and the different colored bell peppers. Brush them with 2 tablespoons of olive oil.

3. Oil the grill grates with 1 teaspoon of olive oil and grill the vegetable skewers for 5 minutes. Flip the skewers and grill for 5 minutes more, or until they are cooked to your liking.

4. Let the skewers cool for 5 minutes before serving.

Per Serving

Calories: 115 | fat: 3.0g | protein: 3.5g | carbs: 18.7g | fiber: 4.7g | sodium: 12mg

Stuffed Portobello Mushroom with Tomatoes

Prep time:

10 minutes | Cook time: 15 minutes | Serves 4

Ingredients

4 large portobello mushroom caps

3 tablespoons extra-virgin olive oil

Salt and freshly ground black pepper, to taste

4 sun-dried tomatoes

1 cup shredded mozzarella cheese, divided

½ to ¾ cup low-sodium tomato sauce

Directions

1. Preheat the broiler to High.

2. Arrange the mushroom caps on a baking sheet and drizzle with olive oil.

1. Sprinkle with salt and pepper.

2. Broil for 1o minutes, flipping the mushroom caps halfway through, until browned on the top.

3. Remove from the broil. Spoon 1 tomato, 2 tablespoons of cheese, and 2 to 3 tablespoons of sauce onto each mushroom cap.

4. Return the mushroom caps to the broiler and continue broiling for 2 to 3 minutes.

5. Cool for 5 minutes before serving.

Per Serving

Calories: 217 | fat: 15.8g | protein: 11.2g | carbs: 11.7g | fiber: 2.0g | sodium: 243mg

Wilted Dandelion Greens with Sweet Onion

Prep time:

15 minutes | Cook time: 15 minutes | Serves 4

Ingredients

1 tablespoon extra-virgin olive oil

2 garlic cloves, minced

1 Vidalia onion, thinly sliced

½ cup low-sodium vegetable broth

2 bunches dandelion greens, roughly chopped

Freshly ground black pepper, to taste

Directions

1. Heat the olive oil in a large skillet over low heat.

2. Add the garlic and onion and cook for 2 to 3 minutes, stirring occasionally, or until the onion is translucent.

3. Fold in the vegetable broth and dandelion greens and cook for 5 to 7 minutes until wilted, stirring frequently.

4. Sprinkle with the black pepper and serve on a plate while warm.

Per Serving

Calories: 81 | fat: 3.9g | protein: 3.2g | carbs: 10.8g | fiber: 4.0g | sodium: 72mg

Celery and Mustard Greens

Prep time:

10 minutes | Cook time: 15 minutes | Serves 4

Ingredients

½ cup low-sodium vegetable broth

1 celery stalk, roughly chopped

½ sweet onion, chopped

½ large red bell pepper, thinly sliced

2 garlic cloves, minced

1 bunch mustard greens, roughly chopped

Directions

1. Pour the vegetable broth into a large cast iron pan and bring it to a simmer over medium heat.

2. Stir in the celery, onion, bell pepper, and garlic. Cook uncovered for about 3 to 5 minutes, or until the onion is softened.

3. Add the mustard greens to the pan and stir well. Cover, reduce the heat to low, and cook for an additional 10 minutes, or until the liquid is evaporated and the greens are wilted.

4. Remove from the heat and serve warm.

Per Serving (1 cup)

Calories: 39 | fat: 0g | protein: 3.1g | carbs: 6.8g | fiber: 3.0g | sodium: 120mg

Vegetable and Tofu Scramble

Prep time:

5 minutes | Cook time: 10 minutes | Serves 2

Ingredients

2 tablespoons extra-virgin olive oil

½ red onion, finely chopped

1 cup chopped kale

8 ounces (227 g) mushrooms, sliced

8 ounces (227 g) tofu, cut into pieces

2 garlic cloves, minced

Pinch red pepper flakes

½ teaspoon sea salt

⅛ teaspoon freshly ground black pepper

Directions

1. Heat the olive oil in a medium nonstick skillet over medium-high heat until shimmering.

2. Add the onion, kale, and mushrooms to the skillet and cook for about 5 minutes, stirring occasionally, or until the vegetables start to brown.

3. Add the tofu and stir-fry for 3 to 4 minutes until softened.

4. Stir in the garlic, red pepper flakes, salt, and black pepper and cook for 30 seconds.

5. Let the mixture cool for 5 minutes before serving.

Per Serving

Calories: 233 | fat: 15.9g | protein: 13.4g | carbs: 11.9g | fiber: 2.0g | sodium: 672mg

Zoodles

Prep time:

10 minutes | Cook time: 5 minutes | Serves 2

Ingredients

2 tablespoons avocado oil

2 medium zucchini, spiralized

¼ teaspoon salt

Freshly ground black pepper, to taste

Directions

1. Heat the avocado oil in a large skillet over medium heat until it shimmers.

2. Add the zucchini noodles, salt, and black pepper to the skillet and toss to coat. Cook for 1 to 2 minutes, stirring constantly, until tender.

3. Serve warm.

Per Serving

Calories: 128 | fat: 14.0g | protein: 0.3g | carbs: 0.3g | fiber: 0.1g | sodium: 291mg

Lentil and Tomato Collard Wraps

Prep time:

15 minutes | Cook time: 0 minutes | Serves 4

Ingredients

2 cups cooked lentils

5 Roma tomatoes, diced

½ cup crumbled feta cheese

10 large fresh basil leaves, thinly sliced

¼ cup extra-virgin olive oil

1 tablespoon balsamic vinegar

2 garlic cloves, minced

½ teaspoon raw honey

½ teaspoon salt

¼ teaspoon freshly ground black pepper

4 large collard leaves, stems removed

Directions

1. Combine the lentils, tomatoes, cheese, basil leaves, olive oil, vinegar, garlic, honey, salt, and black pepper in a large bowl and stir until well blended.

2. Lay the collard leaves on a flat work surface. Spoon the equal-sized amounts of the lentil mixture onto the edges of the leaves. Roll them up and slice in half to serve.

Per Serving

Calories: 318 | fat: 17.6g | protein: 13.2g | carbs: 27.5g | fiber: 9.9g | sodium: 475mg

Stir-Fry Baby Bok Choy

Prep time:

12 minutes | Cook time: 10 to 13 minutes | Serves 6

Ingredients

2 tablespoons coconut oil

1 large onion, finely diced

2 teaspoons ground cumin

1-inch piece fresh ginger, grated

1 teaspoon ground turmeric

½ teaspoon salt

12 baby bok choy heads, ends trimmed and sliced lengthwise

Water, as needed

3 cups cooked brown rice

Directions

1. Heat the coconut oil in a large pan over medium heat.

2. Saut é the onion for 5 minutes, stirring occasionally, or until the onion is translucent.

3. Fold in the cumin, ginger, turmeric, and salt and stir to coat well.

4. Add the bok choy and cook for 5 to 8 minutes, stirring occasionally, or until the bok choy is tender but crisp. You can add 1 tablespoon of water at a time, if the skillet gets dry until you finish sautéing.

5. Transfer the bok choy to a plate and serve over the cooked brown rice.

Per Serving

Calories: 443 | fat: 8.8g | protein: 30.3g | carbs: 75.7g | fiber: 19.0g | sodium: 1289mg

Sweet Pepper Stew

Prep time:

20 minutes | Cook time: 50 minutes | Serves 2

Ingredients

2 tablespoons olive oil

2 sweet peppers, diced (about 2 cups)

½ large onion, minced

1 garlic clove, minced

1 tablespoon gluten-free Worcestershire sauce

1 teaspoon oregano

1 cup low-sodium tomato juice

1 cup low-sodium vegetable stock

¼ cup brown rice

¼ cup brown lentils

Salt, to taste

Directions

1. In a Dutch oven, heat the olive oil over medium-high heat.

2. Sauté the sweet peppers and onion for 10 minutes, stirring occasionally, or until the onion begins to turn golden and the peppers are wilted.

3. Stir in the garlic, Worcestershire sauce, and oregano and cook for 30 seconds more. Add the tomato juice, vegetable stock, rice, and lentils to the Dutch oven and stir to mix well.

4. Bring the mixture to a boil and then reduce the heat to medium-low. Let it simmer covered for about 45 minutes, or until the rice is cooked through and the lentils are tender.

5. Sprinkle with salt and serve warm.

Per Serving

Calories: 378 | fat: 15.6g | protein: 11.4g | carbs: 52.8g | fiber: 7.0g | sodium: 391mg

Alphabetical Index

M

P

R

S

V

W

Z

CPSIA information can be obtained
at www.ICGtesting.com
Printed in the USA
BVHW011158170521
607543BV00007B/1044

9 781802 837773